Color the picture of this sledding a⬚

Use the pictures and word list to complete the puzzle.

Word List
BOOTS
COAT
HAT
MITTENS
SCARF
SWEATER

Across

2.

5.

6.

Down

1.

3.

4.

Unscramble the winter words. Then, unscramble the letters in the snowflakes to solve the riddle.

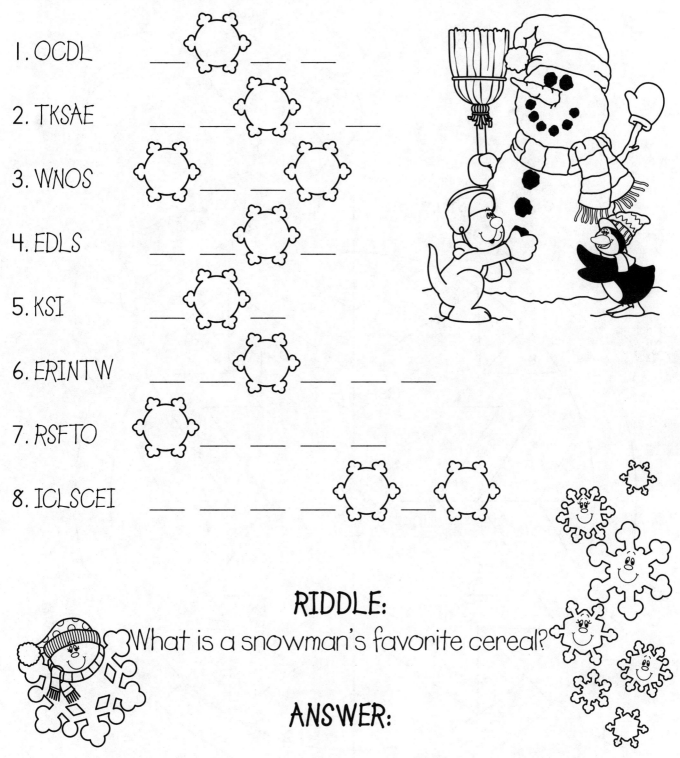

1. OCDL   ___ ⬡ ___ ___

2. TKSAE   ___ ___ ⬡ ___ ___

3. WNOS   ⬡ ___ ___ ⬡

4. EDLS   ___ ___ ⬡ ___

5. KSI   ___ ⬡ ___

6. ERINTW   ___ ___ ___ ⬡ ___ ___

7. RSFTO   ⬡ ___ ___ ___ ___

8. ICLSCEI   ___ ___ ___ ⬡ ___ ⬡ ___ ___

RIDDLE:
What is a snowman's favorite cereal?

ANSWER:

___ ___ ___ ___ ___ ___ ___ ___

Follow the path through the snowflake to its center.

Start

Finish

These cool crafts are for the birds!

Edible Feeder

1. Have an adult punch a small hole through the top of a rice cake.
2. Thread a sturdy string through the hole and make a loop for hanging.
3. Cover the rice cake with peanut butter.
4. Press the rice cake into a plate of birdseed.
5. Hang the feeder on a tree or bush.

Bird Food Garland

1. Gather popcorn, cubes of cheese, and small pieces of fruits and raw vegetables.
2. Have an adult help you thread a blunt needle with heavy-duty thread and tie a knot at the end.
3. Carefully string the food items on the thread and tie a knot at the other end.
4. Hang the garland in a tree or bush.

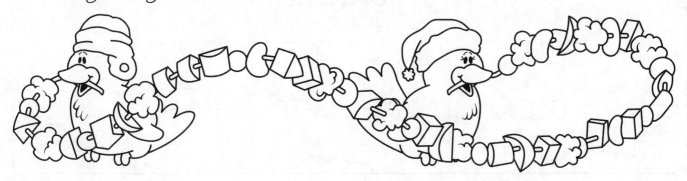

Find and circle the ice-skating words from the word list.

```
    L G N T W I R L
  W F Q B C L P L A K E
  I D A Y S K A T E X F L X
U H G L W Z N C H K B V J F F D
O O W L S U I E O I C I T F O N
  E I F P E G S L H U C K O M O
  F U I F L G L I D E B O
  Z N K W X F M E G
```

Word List

FALL   ICE   LAKE   SPIN

GLIDE   LACES   SKATE   TWIRL

Make a snow mobile!

1. Cut out the snowflake patterns below.
2. Punch a hole near the top of each snowflake.
3. Glue two pencils or craft sticks together to form an X.
4. Use different lengths of thread to tie the snowflakes to the center and ends of the X.

Find and circle 9 animals hidden in the snowy woods.

Connect the dots to see a frosty friend. Start at the ★.

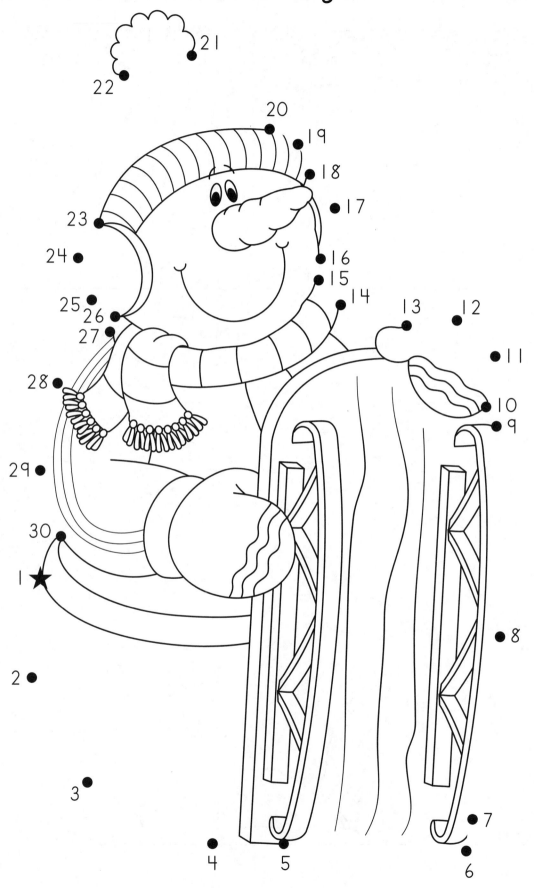

Circle the letter under the correct heading for each word. Then, write the circled letters in order to answer the question.

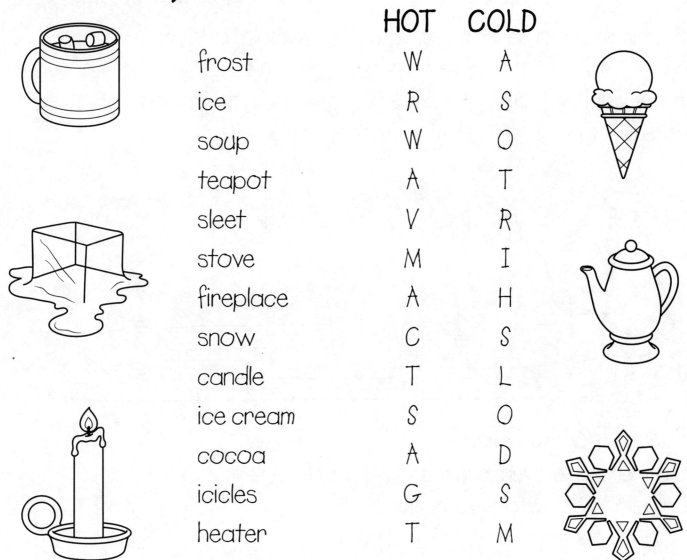

	HOT	COLD
frost	W	A
ice	R	S
soup	W	O
teapot	A	T
sleet	V	R
stove	M	I
fireplace	A	H
snow	C	S
candle	T	L
ice cream	S	O
cocoa	A	D
icicles	G	S
heater	T	M

QUESTION:
How does your bed feel on a cold winter night?

ANSWER:

___ ___ ___ ___   ___ ___ ___ ___ ___   ___ ___ ___

___ ___ ___ ___ ___ ___

Play these cool games to stay warm on a winter day!

Snowball Toss

Sit in a circle with several friends. Place a bucket in the center of the circle. Each person will need a snowball made from crumpled white paper. At the same time, everyone tries to toss her snowball in the bucket. If a player does not get his snowball in the bucket, he is out. Continue playing until one winner is left.

Snow Tracks Race

Gather some friends in a snowy yard or field. Break into two teams and mark a start and a finish line. The first person on each team will run from the start to the finish. Then, each teammate must run to the finish in the same tracks that the first person left. If someone goes out of the tracks, he must start over. The first team to have all players reach the finish wins.

Use the word list and clues to complete the puzzle.

Word List

BOBSLED
HOCKEY
SKATING
SKIING
SLED
SNOWBOARDING
SNOWMOBILE
SNOWSHOES

Across

1. You could use _____ to walk across snow.
4. _____ is like surfing on the snow.
7. Ice- _____ is done on frozen water.

Down

2. Riding a _____ is a fast and fun way to get down a snowy hill.
3. You need a stick and a puck to play ice _____.
4. Gliding down a mountain with two long boards on your feet is called _____.
5. A _____ has metal runners that help it slide down a curvy track.
6. A _____ uses a motor to travel through the snow.

Use the pictures to sound out these wintry words.

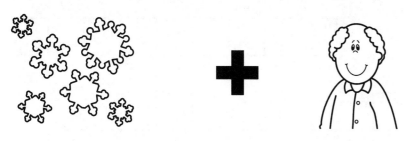

_____

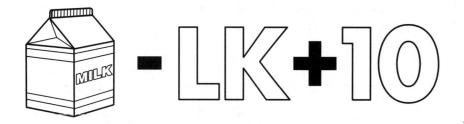

_____

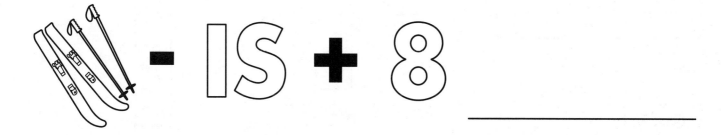

_____

_____

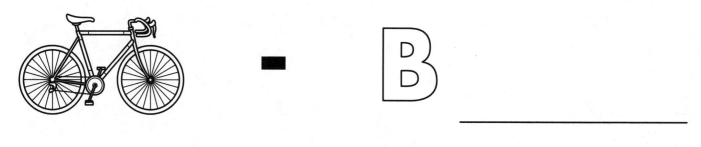

_____

_____

Make this fun ice-skater flip book.

1. Cut out each page of the book.
2. Stack the pages with page 1 on top and staple along the left side.
3. Hold the book in your left hand, flip the pages from front to back with your right thumb, and watch him go!

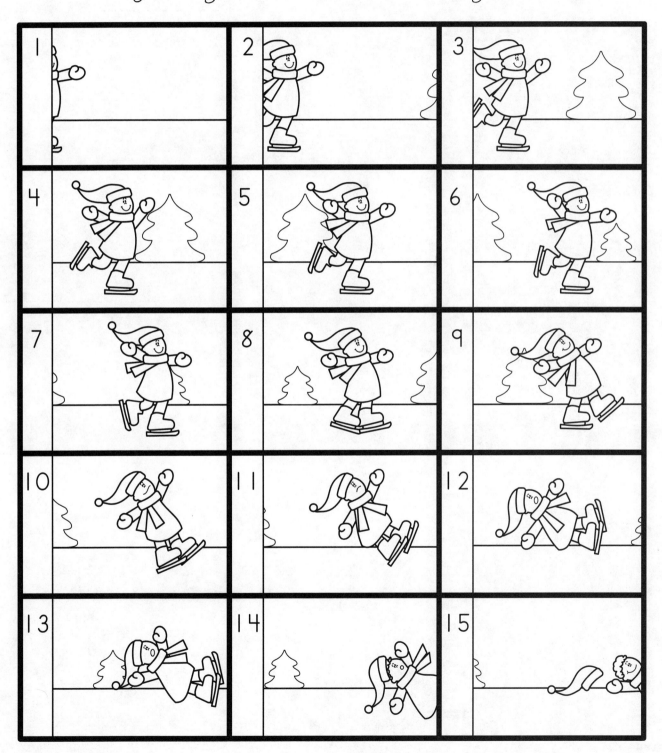

Color the two matching snowmen the same. Color the other snowmen differently.

Help the snowplow clear the path to the house.

Finish

Start

Use the word list to help you decide who or what made each set of tracks in the snow. Then, write each name under the correct tracks.

Word List

bird   child   dog

car   deer   rabbit

Find and circle 12 things that are wrong with this winter fun scene.

Follow the directions to make a yummy winter snack!

| 1 Gather one small and two large rice cakes. | 2 Spread cream cheese or vanilla frosting on top of each rice cake. | 3 Arrange the rice cakes on a plate so they form a snowman. |
| 4 Use raisins, nuts, or candies to make a mouth, eyes, and buttons. | 5 Use pretzel sticks for arms and a small carrot stick for a nose. | 6 Sprinkle with sugar to make the "snow" sparkle. |

Find and circle 10 mittens hidden in the picture.

Follow the directions to cut out a snowflake.

1. Cut out the square.
2. Fold along fold 1.
3. Fold along fold 2.
4. Fold in half and cut out all shaded parts. Open the snowflake.

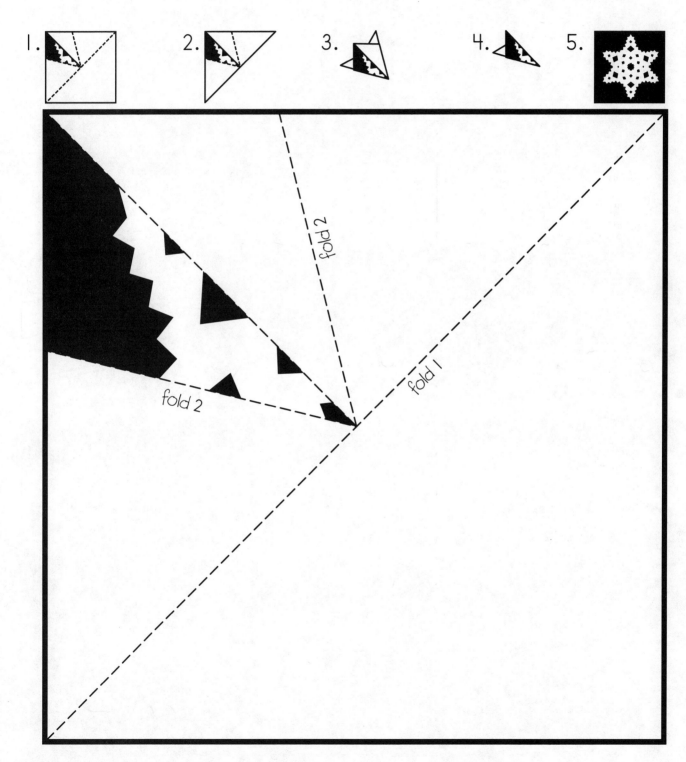

Color by number to see a pretty winter animal.

1 = red   2 = orange   3 = black   4 = blue   5 = brown

Use the word list to complete the puzzle. The first word is done to help you get started.

Word List

3 letters
HAT
ICE
SKI

4 letters
COLD
SLED
SNOW

5 letters
COCOA
SCARF
SKATE

6 letters
FREEZE
ICICLE
MITTEN
SHIVER
WINTER

M I T T E N

Use this snowy dough to build an indoor snowman!

1 Gather soap flakes, water, a large bowl, and an electric mixer.	**2** Combine 4 cups of soap flakes and $1/2$ cup of water in the bowl.	**3** Blend the water and soap flakes with the mixer until it makes a dough.
4 Mold the dough into three balls and stack to make a snowman.	**5** Insert a toothpick down the center of the stack to secure.	**6** Decorate the snowman with beads, twigs, and other items.

Find and circle 10 differences between these two wintry scenes.

Find and circle the snowman materials listed in the word list.

Word List
BROOM
BUTTONS
CARROT
COAL
HAT
MITTENS
PIPE
SCARF
SNOW
TWIGS

```
F E C M H R A Z E E
T W Z Q O I N P I P E F
I W J E J W A T E O C O Z I
S G I H S M Y K L T V Z S T G L
U S G N Y W H S S O E X D H S X
L U S N O W E N V D R N B I U F
R P L U P S O S Q E R Y S T D
L K K O O T N B Z K L W V U K L
Z Z B T I E K W H W U G Z Z
P U W V X A C A R R O T
B R O O M F N T N N M S
S C A R F N J G B R
```

Connect the dots to see what Jack Frost has painted on your window.

Color this cozy scene.

Brrr! Keep your cool while you use the clues to find these br- words.

b r ___ ___ ___   You use this to style your hair.

b r ___ ___ ___   Your skull protects this organ.

b r ___ ___ ___   You need this to make a sandwich.

b r ___ ___ ___ ___ ___ ___   A tree has many of these.

b r ___ ___ ___ ___ ___ ___   This is a green vegetable.

b r ___ ___ ___   This is the color of hot chocolate.

b r ___ ___ ___ ___ ___   Your mother's son is called this.

b r ___ ___ ___ ___   This is the opposite of fixed.

b r ___ ___ ___   This helps you clean the floor.

Brrrrr!   Brrrrr!